EVERY MAN HAS ONE:

A DREAM

GLEN M REED

Copyright © 2024 Glen M Reed

Some names and identifying details have been changed to protect the privacy of individuals.

No part of this book may be reproduced, or stored in a retrieval system, or transmitted in any form or by any means, electronic, mechanical, photocopying, recording, or otherwise, without express written permission of the publisher.

All rights reserved.

ISBN: 9798320915173

Table of Contents

Recovery 1

LPN Program 11

40th Birthday 16

Crystal & Smiths' Wedding 48

Eddie 62

60th Birthday 81

Travel Agent 85

Grassroots 93

Don 98

Album 124

Yvette 131

2023 134

Jacksonville.. 137

New Orleans 147

Nicki 154

Goals 166

Expectations 171

Sticking Together 186

Joey 197

Full Circle 202

ACKNOWLEDGMENTS

I want to truly acknowledge Wendy Williams. She's the one that inspired me to write this trilogy. I knew her from St Clair Township. She used to date a classmate of mine, Aaron Rogers. R.I.P She was a freshman, and we were juniors in high school. The Rogers were infamous for their weekend parties and great times!!! I was following Wendy from The

Wendy Williams experience on WBLS from the beginning. I used to call in often, and when she became a best-selling author, I loved her first book. "The Wendy Williams Experience." For the most part, she was really open and honest about her life. So she's the one that inspired me. I went to quite a few of her book signings. I supported her champagne venture and her store on Elm Street, which was in St. Claire. I used to go to the Laugh Factory in New York City when she hosted. Also to the Dons and Divas that she hosted at a couple of different places, so we have a history. Her father, Thomas Williams Senior, is also an author, and I had the pleasure of spending Father's Day at his house in Miami in 2022. He autographed his book that I supported, and we had a really great conversation. I also told him that I was writing a book. God bless his soul; he's going to be 92 this year. I'm really hoping and praying that Wendy's is in a good place. She kind of fell off the radar, and every time I asked about her, they said she was doing fine, so hopefully and prayerfully, it's true. I will continue praying for her to have a healthy recovery, peace, and blessings to her and her family…Love You, Wendy!!!

THE DREAM

Wendy Williams at her first book signing "The Wendy Williams Experience"

THE DREAM

Wendy & I at a function

THE DREAM

Wendy's second book signing

RECOVERY

Now, you must be thinking, what the hell happened to Maurice? Cops were standing in my living room, guns pointed at us, Artie was frozen, looking crazy, and I was on the ground handcuffed, looking up at him, and the crazy ass cops were still yelling at Artie, "GET DOWN! GET DOWN ON THE GROUND!"

Well, they hauled our asses out to the front backyard, and there was Ant and Troy sitting on the ground handcuffed. They dragged them out of the first-floor apartment building, so they raided both places at the same time. All four of us were sitting there handcuffed, and I guess the head detective that was on the take and screwing the crackhead girl was asking all these questions, "So where is it? Where's all the stuff? You better tell us." As he was saying that, this young black cop was escorting Glen out the door, saying, "You need to tell us where everything is unless your brother is going to go down too." "Oh shit, Where the fuck did he come from?" Oh my God, I forgot all about

Glen. He was in the room taking a nap while all this shit was going down! "What shit? What are you talking about"? "I don't have nothing," I protested. I looked up at Glen, who was still half asleep and discombobulated. In that second, I felt like shit because I forgot all about him.

The officers were still screaming and shouting out, "Where's the stuff"? Where are all your drugs?" Again, I shouted back at them, "I don't know what the hell you're talking about. I don't have no damn drugs." Now, mind you, those Pig bastards had been staking out my spot for a minute and then knocked down doors and raided two spots. Both the front and back apartments. I don't know how much manpower they had, but they thought they were making a big grand bust, and all they got was a crackhead drug user and drug-selling person with six vials of coke. "Oh, oh, what? Are you referring to these six vials that I have in my pocket here? Yeah, go on, take 'em,'" I said with a smirk on my face. "You slimy fucking PIGS," I was thinking to myself. Well, needless to say, we were all hauled Uptown, fingerprinted, and put into a holding cell. Now, mind you; they would not let me put on shoes or a shirt, so I was freezing to death in that fucking cell. But I knew they were pissed off because they found absolutely nothing, and then they made up this whole big story like they made this huge bust.

The day that I read that story in The Star-Ledger and the St. Clair Township local paper, I vowed never to believe shit I ever read again. Because, again, they always put the narrative in their favor. Those slimy pieces of shit found six vials of cocaine on me, but the paper read that they found $3,200, like a hundred vitals of cocaine, and all this paraphernalia. They blew the story up like they always do. Lies, lies, lies. Those cops were dirty, just like the majority of them. They didn't have a warrant. My third-floor tenant Pop F.W. (R.I.P.,) had told me that they were tearing that place up trying to find drugs, and he told me they were pissed. He can hear them talking and getting pissed by the minute. But their trifling asses didn't mention the $675 they stole because Pop had just paid the rent, and I put it in the drawer. That wasn't on the police report, you thieving bastards!!!

    Glen was released a few hours after he got up there because he honestly had nothing to do with it; he was an innocent bysleeper. But of course, they called each person up one by one. They called me last. They were trying to get us to rat each other out and find out what each person knew about anything. I never asked the other guys what they said or what they didn't say, but when they called me up and were

THE DREAM

Interrogating me, telling me all this bullshit that I was going down, and I was getting all these years. I just said to them, "I'm sick, and I need help. I'm a crackhead. I don't know what the hell you're talking about."

So, of course, again, they were pissed the hell off even more. It was a little six-vial cocaine bust, and they probably spent a shitload of money with the manpower they had to hire to watch my place or whatever they did. Half of them were on the payroll of the real drug dealers who were getting in and out of jail every other day, so they knew the deal anyway. I was no big-time drug dealer.

We were arraigned 5 or 6 days later, and I had to appear in front of the judge. "How do you plead?" the judge asked. "Guilty, your honor. With an explanation if I may." I looked like a sick, disheveled homeless person who hadn't bathed or brushed his teeth for six days, so I used it to my advantage. "Your honor, I started smoking crack cocaine and lost my mind, and I need help," I pleaded to the judge. I was sentenced to 6 months probation and an outpatient program for 28 days.

The first week of the program and being clean was very rough. It took some adjusting, some soul searching, some dedication, and determination. The NA (Narcotic Anonymous) and AA (Alcohol Anonymous) programs work if you work the program, and I have to admit I didn't do all the steps they told me to do. Like 90 meetings in 90 days and a whole bunch of stuff that I didn't quite make. The NA meetings would entice me to want to get high and use, so I started going to AA meetings. A lot of the principles are the same, but the war stories are different. I use all the tools necessary to make this journey successful for me. One day at a time, people, places, things, and a higher power in my life: that's what sustains me. And living life on life's terms. It's not always a pretty picture, but it's real. I've been clean and sober for 26 years, this August 21, 2023.

THE DREAM

LPN PROGRAM

I haven't been to a meeting in probably 10 to 15 years. I've been navigating through life differently, but I truly know that I can't pick up again. I don't need to drink again, and I know that deep in my SOUL!!! I'm not saying I would never go to a meeting; it just isn't part of my lifestyle or routine. I did say I was going to go speak and try to give back. And it still may be in the cards, but I live a pretty productive life.

After becoming clean and sober on August 21, 1997, I was a shoe salesman for Macy's for a year. From 1998 to 2001, I was a shoe salesman for Lord & Taylor, and I was the highest shoe salesman for three years. Even after they set me up to get fired. From that experience, I realized I had to become self-sufficient and explore the entrepreneurial realm. I started taking care of my best friend Jim's dad. I would go over in the morning and get him dressed and feed him breakfast, drive him to adult daycare, then pick him up, feed him dinner, get him ready for bed, and do the same routine the next day. I realized I didn't have anyone to answer to. I did my job, I took care of Mr. Lewis, and everything was good. In that moment, I realized I enjoyed taking care of people, and I could make this my thing. A career. Within a couple of weeks, I took a home health aide course, and then I started nursing school (LPN program) a couple of years later at Essex County College in Newark, New Jersey. I went on to do private-duty nursing for over 25 years. I worked with over 40 or 50 families within that time span.

One of my favorite families to work for was the Stick family from Madison, New Jersey. Mr John Stick was my patient. I miss that old man. He was a very frail, tall white man. I had gotten him through an agency, but I managed to get him on my own full-time. I wrote out a proposal to his son, who was paying me, and he paid me very well. Before John's health took a turn for the worse, he was very self-sufficient, and he enjoyed doing upholstery work. He had some really nice pieces of furniture that he was working on before he got sick. We had a great relationship. I took care of him for about a year and a half, I think. From that, his family and I became really close. They really liked me, and I really cared a lot about them. Actually, I just spoke to Jess and Al this year. They're doing well, and they're happy grandparents of, I believe, 13 grandkids, she told me. That's great and she is still doing her photography thing. Mr. John Stick's memory will always be close to me because he had two favorite words that he would use all the time: "mercy and dreadful." For instance, any given morning when I would walk in and go into the bedroom, I would say, "Good Morning. How are you feeling today?" His reply was, "Oh mercy, I feel dreadful," if we were watching the news. "Oh mercy, that's dreadful," was his saying. At one point, I had my whole family saying it in his memory…I miss him.

40TH BIRTHDAY

In November 2001, I threw myself a 40th birthday party. I had been clean for three years and change. Over 100 people were in attendance, and it was a beautiful time. I was just so proud of myself for becoming the human being that I knew I could become.

THE DREAM

I ended up getting my second client, Ms.CC. Cassandra was a singer and a background singer, for many artists. and she was good friends with Jim's sister, but she ended up breaking her ankle. So, by word of mouth, she ended up calling me, and I worked for her for over ten years. Through that employment, I became acquainted and good friends with Nick Ashford and Valerie Simpson. So, for over ten years, from 2002 - 2012, I was rubbing elbows and becoming friendly with some legendary folks. Dr. Maya Angelou, Quincy Jones, Patti Labelle, Freddie Jackson, Meli'sa Morgan, Allison Williams, Mo'Nique Ledisi, John Stanley. Just to name a few. Nick and Val owned "The Sugar Bar," a restaurant on 72nd Street in New York City, and I frequented it almost every Thursday when I was in town. You never knew who you would run into or meet at open mic.

Thursday nights were infamous for the Sugar Bar. I was up in the Cat Lounge, sitting at the table having dinner with Nick, and somebody was performing. I would be singing the song, and Nick would say, "When are you going to take your behind on that stage and sing for me?" I still felt pretty confident and knew my voice was decent but that stage fright thing is real. Plus, the stage there was small, and the lights made it hot, so I never did it. One day, maybe. One day, for you, Nick. But I always held that close to my heart when Nick Ashford told me I could sing!!! Another moment that was legendary and that I hold close to my heart was when Tee called me and set up an interview with Dr. Maya Angelou. Oh yes, I had the pleasure of interviewing with Dr. Maya Angelou on two different occasions. Both were at her beautiful Brownstone in Harlem on Lenox Avenue. She wanted me to live in The Brownstone. She just wanted a male presence in and out on a daily basis. My boy C.W., who I would be replacing, was going to the west coast to Cali to better his acting career. Dr. Angelou, at this point, would be in the New York City area four or five times a year, but she wanted me to be there in case she was hosting dignitaries like Coretta Scott King or, for whatever reason, she needed me. She was having a lot of knee issues at this time, so she was telling me that she might need me to be a sous chef or to help her out in the kitchen because Dr. Angelou could cook, and she loved to do so. Well, a week or two went by, and I was called in for a second interview. Well, needless to say, I didn't get the job. At one point during the interview, I realized I wasn't qualified for the job. Or to her liking. Dr Angelou was old school. She carried herself with dignity and Grace and I just wasn't polished enough at that point, and I was keen enough to understand that. But my Ego really wanted to work for the legendary Dr. Maya Angelou.

I guess it was about five or ten minutes into the interview that the doorbell rang. Lydia, Dr Angelou's right-hand woman, announced that such and such a person was here. I can't remember this woman's name for the life of me, but I believe she was a known author. At this point, Dr. Angelou says to Lydia, "You better tell her to come in here and give me some love." Then, the woman proceeded to walk into the area where we were. Now, mind you, my back is facing the woman approaching us. I was sitting across from Dr. Angelou, so as this woman approached, I turned in my seat to greet her, and when she was right by my side, I said, "Hello, I'm Maurice. Nice to meet you." But I never stood up. So Dr. Angelou and this woman had their moment. They hug and kiss hello, chat for a minute, and then say their goodbyes. Then, the woman leaves. After she is gone, Dr. Angelou READS me, with only that distinctive, deep, undeniable voice of hers. ... She leans in, looks me dead in my eyes, and boom, "MAURICE. YOU MUST ALWAYS STAND WHEN A WOMAN ENTERS A ROOM!!" And I was like, "Oh shit," in my head. I apologized. and told her I was very sorry and that she was absolutely right. At that moment, I realized I needed to be more polished in etiquette training, so I knew I wasn't fit for the job. Lesson learned. But the best interview ever because, again, I was in the presence of a legend. A couple of weeks later, I ran into Tee at the Sugar Bar and asked if Dr. Angelou had found anyone to fill the position, and he told me it was an elderly couple, so I didn't feel so bad.

I had the pleasure of seeing Dr. Angelou three or four times after that. Unfortunately, the next time I saw Dr. Angelo was at Nick and Val's house a couple of nights after Nick had passed (R.I.P.) I had cooked some food and took it over to the house as they were preparing for the funeral. Dr. Angelo had planned to attend, but she was a little under the weather herself, so I helped Frank escort her to the car. She was weak and on oxygen, and she was taking Nick's passing pretty badly. I told her that I loved her and that I would see her tomorrow, but I never got a chance to because she didn't make the funeral. So Felicia Rashad and a couple of other ladies read some poems that Dr. Angelou was planning to recite.

Nick's homegoing celebration was absolutely beautiful. Truly sad but very inspiring and very uplifting. Freddie Jackson sang, Tanisha Arnold sang…just a beautiful and powerful service. I have so many wonderful stories and great memories of meeting Legends at the Sugar Bar. I hadn't been there in over ten years because I moved to Atlanta, but I stopped by a couple of times this year. It's still fun, still happening, but they close a little earlier because of that crazy pandemic (COVID). But it's still thriving. Val still comes on Thursdays and sings background for the patrons who get up on the stage. She looks great and sounds great. I was in the Garden Room that Thursday promoting my books, and this young lady and I were chatting. I asked her if she was singing tonight, and she told me yes. I told her about my wanting to sing and that I sang for Nick years ago. I felt pretty confident about my voice, but I just wasn't ready to hit the stage yet. She was giving me some confidence, and I almost did it, but I didn't take the extra step. But, she got up there, and she tore that song up. Beautiful voice, beautiful young lady. She got up on stage and sanggg!!!

Over the ten-year span that I hung out at the Sugar Bar, I brought hundreds of family and friends to that spot. It was just a great place to vibe on a Thursday night. Great times!!! Even though ten years prior, I had my 50th birthday party, and I invited 70 people from the Sugar Bar to my party. None of them showed up. Now, of course, Val gets a pass because Nick had just transitioned that August, and my birthday party was in November, but it's just something about New Yorkers leaving the city to head to New Jersey. They don't really do it. It's kind of taboo, very strange, very weird, and

rude, but I've grown and moved on.

Me and Jackie at Nick and Val's White Party 2005

THE DREAM

Mo'nique handing at the Sugar Bar

Me and Tracy Morgan at the Village Underground

"Open Mic Night"

THE DREAM

Ron Grant, me, my sister, and my nephew

Lynn Whitfield and I…Just another Thursday Night at Nick and Val's Sugar Bar

THE DREAM

Me and the beautiful Lynn Whitfield hanging at The Sugar Bar in NYC

Me and The Legendary Maya Angelou

THE DREAM

Actress Robin Givens and me at Thursday night "Open Mic Night" at the Sugar Bar

Legendary Nick Ashford and Valerie Simpson

THE DREAM

Me and my dear friend Nick Ashford

Nick and I up in the "Cat Lounge" holding it down

THE DREAM

Freddy Jackson, Meli'sa Morgan, Nick, and I

Freddy, Nick, and Val on stage signing their butts off!

THE DREAM

Wallce, Mel'isa Morgan, and me

Mario and me

THE DREAM

Nick and Val's Legendary White Party! Dr. Maya Angelou

Freddy and I

THE DREAM

Ann, Mel'isa, and me

All the folks in their white, poolside

THE DREAM

Me and Val

Nick Ashford and Val Simpson

THE DREAM

White Party at Nik and Val's, poolside

THE DREAM

Val, her brother Ray "The Police" in the Village People, Nick, and Jimmy

Cindy Lauper, singing her heart out

THE DREAM

Queen Latifa and me at the Sugar Bar

Fantasia hanging out at the Sugar Bar

THE DREAM

Chaz Shepherd and me

Me and Freddy Jackson

THE DREAM

Me and Tatyana Ali hanging out at the Sugar Bar

THE DREAM

Nick and Val serenading the crowd at the Sugar Bar

Happy Birthday to me! Val serenading me

THE DREAM

Nick thinking he's getting some of my cake. Not!

Andrea, Val, and me celebrating my birthday

THE DREAM

Master P, his daughter "Niq" and Romeo at the Black American Film Festival in Miami 2019

THE DREAM

Romeo and me at the B.A.F.F. in Miami 2019

Tobias Truvllion and me

THE DREAM

Lahmard Tate and me at the B.A.F.F. in Miami 2019

CRYSTAL & SMITHS' WEDDING

Thinking back, I realized that the last time I laid eyes on Cassie was during my trip to Paris. I left a lock on the bridge, so I have to take another trip to see if I can find it. Crystal was an excellent tour guide and gave us the rundown on everything there was to see in the city. At the time, I knew Crystal had been seeing someone for the Caribbean. Things must have been moving pretty quickly because they got engaged six months later. I had heard her talk about him on a couple of different occasions, but I finally met him one day in New York City. His name is Smith, and he was a singer/musician on a ship, Princess Cruise Line. They were going to be docked in the city for the weekend, so Crystal invited us to take a tour of the ship, have lunch, hang out, and meet her fiancé. So Crystal, her roommate Ally, and I drove over to the city that beautiful Saturday afternoon and met up with Smith. He gave us a tour of the ship, which was very nice, and then

THE DREAM

we had a really lovely buffet lunch. We sat around and chopped it up, and that's when Crystal announced that they were getting married in the fall of September.

I had the pleasure of being an usher at Smith and Crystal's wedding but the more exciting part for me was seeing Cassie. She wasn't in the wedding. She was more behind the scenes but very involved. The last time I physically laid eyes on Cassie was in Paris. We spoke on the phone briefly a couple of times, but she's very busy with work, and I was traveling a lot, so our paths just never crossed. She looked absolutely beautiful. She had on this black beaded shimmery type cocktail dress that came right below her thigh, makeup done perfectly with a beautiful lipstick tone, just looking like I wanted to eat her up. I couldn't wait for the wedding to be over so the reception could start. I was looking all over for Cassie, but she was nowhere in sight. Like I said, I guess she was handling stuff behind the scenes but I was hoping to at least get a dance in or something.

The wedding was nice, and the food was good. The drinks were flowing, and everybody seemed to be having a great time, but I was bummed out because Cassie had just disappeared. I text her a couple of times with no reply. It was about 11:30 pm, and we had to be out of the reception hall by midnight, so I just kind of took off towards the elevator to head up to my room. When I turned the corner, I saw Cassie getting into the elevator. I couldn't believe my eyes, so I ran, but it was too late. The elevated door had closed. I just stood there dumbfounded, but then I looked up to see what floor it stopped on. It was the fourth floor, the same floor I was on. Then the elevator started to proceed back down, so I knew it had to be her getting off on the 4th floor. The elevator behind me opened. I pushed the four buttons on the elevator frantically, hoping the door would hurry up and close and that I would make it up there before she got into her room.

THE DREAM

As the door opened, I jumped off the bed. I look to my right, then my left, and I see nothing, but I hear a voice a little distance away, around the corner. I hauled ass down the hall, and when I turned the corner, I saw Cassie entering the room right next to mine. "Holy shit, I can't believe her room is right next to me. This is fate," I'm thinking to myself. So I walked up to room 468, and I kind of stood in front of the door for a second contemplating what to do, but I had to see her, so I tapped on the door, and it opened. "Hey Maurice, what are you doing here?" "Hey, Cassie. I know you're not going to believe this, but we're neighbors. I'm in room 4 6999, and your 4 6888 isn't that ironic," I said, smiling and giggling just a little bit. She retorted back, "Oh yeah, 68, and I owe you one," and she opened the door a little wider for me to step in.

I hugged her and took a quick peck on the cheek and lips, and she invited me in. "Come on in, have a seat. Can I get you some water or anything to drink?" she asked. "I'll have water, thanks." Cassie handed me some water, poured herself a little glass of red wine, then plopped on the bed next to me and gave a big sigh of relief." Are you tired?" I ask. "Tired is not the word. I'm exhausted, and my feet are killing me," she answered back, sounding depleted. "Oh, poor baby. Let me help you with that," I said as I reached down and grabbed both her legs so her feet were in my lap. I started to massage them one at a time. "Oh my GOD, Mo, damn, that feels great," she yells out as she's laying on her back looking up at the ceiling, just moaning and groaning in ecstasy while my skilled hands are making love to her feet. This went on for about 10 minutes or so, and she was just laying back chilling, and of course, I was getting all riled up. So I whispered out, "If you like, I can give you a whole body massage." "Oh my God, that would be great. But I don't know, I might fall asleep on you," she answered back. "The way I'm about to make you feel, I doubt that very seriously, but if you drift off, it's no biggie I answered back, hoping that she wouldn't fall asleep.

Cassie stood to her feet and turned her back to me. "Here, Mo, unzip me," she said to me. "Sure, no problem," I replied. As I was standing behind her, I slowly unzipped her dress, but also just took it in, all of her essence. "Wow, you smell delicious," I said as I kissed the back of her neck, and her sexy cocktail dress fell to her ankles. "Hey, listen. Do you have any kind of oil or anything here? If not, I can run next door and get mine," I offered. "Oh no. Go get yours, and just don't shut the door all the way," she says to me as I'm running out the door to get the oil and grab a condom or two, just in case.

"Knock knock. It's me; I'm back," I called out. I was back like in 10 seconds flat. I closed the door behind me and walked towards the bed. Cassie's laying there on her stomach under one sheet, butt-ass naked. I stripped down in two seconds, and crawled onto the bed and said, "Damn woman, I could eat you alive. You look so good." She snapped back and said, "Stop talking and put your mouth where the cookie is." "Shit, you ain't gotta tell me twice." I pulled that sheet off, turned her ass around through those legs up in the air, and started eating that cookie like it was my last meal.

THE DREAM

"Hmm hmm, Cassie, damn, I miss this," I said as I was down there pleasuring her clit and tasting all her womanly juices. "Shit, MO, OH YESS WORK DAT TONGUE OHHH YEAH YOUUU GOT MEE SOO WET, IT FEELS SOOO GOOD!!! I brought Cassie to a clitorial orgasm with my cunnilingus skills, but Mr. Anaconda was ready to punch in and get to work. I slipped on my condom and whispered in Cassie's ear, "Are you ready for it, baby? Do you want it now?" "Yes, MO, I want it. Give IT to me," she called out. Her juices were flowing so heavily down there that Mr. Anaconda went in with ease. Her warm woman vessel grasped onto Mr. Anaconda, and it was the perfect fit.

THE DREAM

The perfect rhythm. We made love for about 15-20 minutes. We were in that zone, and I just knew we were going to cum together. I was ready. Truth be told, I was probably ready a few minutes before …I held out for her, and I could feel her intensity growing… "OHH YEAH, OOH YESS MO. RIGHT THERE MO, YOU KNOW MY SPOT YESSS YESS OH OH OOOH YEAH DATS IT GIVE IT TOOO MEEEE YESSS MAURICEE YESSS IM CUMMMING BABY!!!!!" OHHH SHIT OOOH YEAH," I said as I collapsed with a big smile on my face. "Oh my GOD, Cassie that was, oh my God, it was great!!! I said as I kissed her on the lips and rolled off of her. She smiled, looked at me, and said, "I thought I was exhausted before. Now I'm just dead." We laughed and fell off to sleep.

Around 6:30 a.m., Cassie was still sleeping peacefully with a little smile on her face. I slipped out of the door, and the coast was clear, so I slid into my room, plopped down on my bed, and just reminisced about what had just taken place a couple of hours ago. She should be awake by now. I had texted her at 9:30 but there was no response, so I went and tapped on her door. No answer. "Damn, I know she couldn't have left without saying goodbye," I was thinking to myself. I went back to my room and dialed her hotel phone. It rang five or six times. "Oh wow, she's gone," I thought. My first instinct was to go downstairs in the lobby to see if I could find her, but then I said, "If it was meant to be, it would be." I had left her a few texts. She has my number, so I'd let her call me.

EDDIE

It was 2006 July fourth when I was going to Crystal & Smiths' house for their annual backyard Shindig. But I wanted to get my midday pick-its in before I went there. I was parking my 10-speed bike right by the entrance of the Exxon station, and as I was putting down the kickstand, this fine young Spanish dude turned the corner with both hands full of shopping bags. Our eyes locked, and I said hello, and he just smiled. I proceeded to go into the store, thinking that he was probably 17 or 18 years old. He looked very young. But very handsome, nice full lips, Beautiful hazel eyes, long eyelashes, a head full of black shiny hair, and short. Probably 5'7".

Anyway, I still thought he was under 21. To my surprise, when I get out outside, I saw him standing by the curb getting ready to cross the street, so I jumped on the bike to catch up to him, and I said to him, "Looks like somebody went shopping" He just looked at me and smiled then I said to myself, oh shit he doesn't speak a bit of English. We crossed the street, then I said to him, "¿Habla español?" "Sí," he replied. "¿Habla inglés?" "No, no. Muy poco," he answered back. Now, I understand Spanish more than I can speak it, but I know the basics. So, I asked his name, "¿Cómo te llamas"? "Mi nombre es Eddie," he replied. "Eddie, my name is Maurice." So then I asked him where he lived. "¿Donde vive?" He pointed to the next block, which was only a block away from Crystal and Smith's house.

Needless to say, we just kept walking, trying to communicate, and we ended up in the park. We sat down on a bench near the stairs by the Glen. What was so intriguing about him was when I spoke to him very slowly, trying to make him understand, that he was looking dead into my eyes. That was turning me on. I finally found out he was 29 years old, so he was way over the legal age. So, it was on and popping then. We were in the park for about an hour and a half, and I realized that I needed to get to the party, and he needed to get back home anyway. I gave him my phone number. I walked him home so I could see exactly which house he lived in, and then I headed off to the party.

Eddie and I ended up being in a five-year relationship. While the first four years were really good, the last year was a struggle. I didn't want to lose him, but he didn't trust me, and if you don't have trust, the relationship is not solid. And when I'm committed to a person, I'm committed to that person, so that was his insecurities that he had to deal with. Things that a lot of people don't understand about relationships is that you can't change an individual; they have to want to make the changes. You cannot make someone trust you; the trust has to be there. I trusted him wholeheartedly. I will leave my phone anywhere because I had nothing to hide, but he was always checking my phone, always asking a million questions. I knew he was a little insecure, but I thought it was because of the language barrier and just being a little uncomfortable because he was foreign. But all my friends knew him, all the people I hung around knew him, and my family loved and adored him. Overall, he's a good human being. He just didn't have that trust factor, and of course, he was the one out there cheating and fooling around. So I ended it.

COVID 19 & BLACK LIVES

February 2020. I was in D.C. taking care of a friend of mine who had a hip replacement. Right at the beginning of this Covid-19 man-made bullshit. It was Pandemonium. The news was giving us all these crazy reports they were shutting stuff down, and everybody was in a panic. The unknown and fear is an unhealthy combination. The news, the CDC, everybody was lying. Nobody had any real facts. It was a hot mess. The only reality that was real to me and others was the number of people that were dying. The numbers were probably played with, I'm sure, but there was a whole bunch of folks dropping dead from this Coronavirus. I've lost a couple of family members, some dear friends, and quite a few people that I know through other people, so it hit home for me seriously. The government's crazy-ass had us in lockdown, afraid to go to the store to leave our house to go to work, to do anything. It was crazy. And every day, the numbers were astronomical, so you knew it was real. You wanted to believe CNN, the CDC, and Anthony Fauci, but when it comes to the government, the political agenda, and the powers that be, they'll say and do anything that works on their behalf. So what if they kill 500,000 people or whatever to get the population in control? Or to win the votes, or whatever it is, they will do it. The government and powers that be do not give a shit about people of color, end of story, period!!! And until we, as a black community, get our shit together and understand that we don't really need the approval of the white Construct. We'll probably be better off as a people. I'm really ready to be segregated again. The only fear is, if we had our thriving communities or an equal opportunity to get homes, to start businesses, to advance as a people, If we had an equal playing field or close to a fair shot, we'd have a fighting chance, but that will NEVER happen. They don't want us to thrive. They want us to stay Suppressed, Oppressed, and Depressed (SOD). They have an agenda, and there always will be a system in place for us black and brown folk. And unfortunately, that is to keep us at the bottom of the totem poll.

Every person and every minority that comes into this country has surpassed us tenfold. They can get assistance, they can get loans, they can get homes, and interest rates lower than us. The system is rigged, and it needs to be torn down and reconstructed, but that will probably never happen in my lifetime.

If you look at Black Wall Street in Tulsa, Oklahoma, in the 1920s, black folks were thriving, black businesses were booming, folks had it going on, and what happened? White folks bombed it and burnt It to the ground. Again, in the 1960s, Black folks were starting to thrive again and had good jobs at the car plants, working on the assembly lines, painters, plumbers, auto mechanics, all those different trades that black folks were making a great living. They had their own businesses and felt a sense of pride and a sense of belonging to Good Ole America, but what did the schools across the USA do? They took all those trades away in the late 70s. Their attitude was, "Oh no, these black folks are doing well. They're coming in our neighborhoods. They're buying our homes. They are almost like equal to us. We got to put a stop to this," and they did. But we didn't catch it. We were too busy thinking that we had to befriend the enemy and move into their space and places, so we were blindsided by the fact that they depleted all the trades to keep us from thriving. So now they take it a step further, they thought, Let's give Negroes an opportunity for a college education. We're going to send them to college. Like they cared! Like they were doing us a favor. So that's when the boom started in the seventies when almost everybody could go to college and get a higher education. We took the bait, hook, line, and sinker. So, the trick was to get us in debt for the rest of our lives. Unfortunately, our black community still believes that education is the best thing for us. Now, don't get me wrong. I believe that education is great, but if you have a trade to fall back on, it's even greater. Because what they did, and what they're still doing, is allowing people to go to college and get those $100,000 and $200,000 dollars loans, so you'll be paying and being in debt for the rest of your life. Wasn't Obama our first black president, and also the first president that I know of, who was in debt from student loans? That's disgusting. A travesty. A lot of us can't see the forest for the trees. They throw us a crumb, and we get all excited and think it's so great. But you have to look at the deeper picture. It's always an agenda when it comes to black and brown people; they do not give a shit about us. Then the plot thickens; they trick us by putting black people in office and then by putting black people on TV. Strategically, mind you. So we will feel like we're starting to fit in, that we belong… and blah blah blah. Then you find out that these black people that we've been looking up to are married to white people. Van Jones, Whoopi Goldberg, Don Lemon, W Kamau Bell, Kamala Harris, and a slew of others. So then the question becomes, are they really down for us? I don't think so.

So when we heard that Kamala Harris was on the ticket, that's all we needed to hear. I bet half of us, or more than half of us, didn't know she was married to a white man till after the fact. We just saw a black sister getting into the White House, and we were sold. I just know that a person who marries into the white structure cannot be down for the black people. It just doesn't work. It's not logical. And, they knew what they were doing. They (the powers that be) are some cunning, downright dirty folk. But a lot of it is our fault. We're easily fooled or easily pleased, and we settle for the bullshit. The other part, too, is that every black person is not down for us, and what I do know is that the political realm is corrupt...so white, black, brown, green, or yellow, I'm not sure if I agree with any of them. I know you have to trust some people, but it's hard. What I do know for sure is that politics is an ole white man's dirty game. They allowed some coons and uncle tom's in the arena, but don't be fooled; they are still in CHARGE!!!

Everything the government and the CDC and the FBI and the CIA try to do. To destroy the black population, it always comes back to bite them in the ass. They get rid of a lot of us, but they also kill their own at the same time. No one on this earth is going to convince me otherwise. That these diseases, drugs, guns, and alcohol weren't a strategic plan to do just that. But the sad part about the people who run this world is they don't mind killing or cheating, even if it's their own, just to stay in control and in charge.

But hopefully, one day, I'm sure not in my lifetime, our black leaders will come together and take back what is rightfully ours because our counterparts lied about everything. They stole everything. That's why they don't want history to be truthfully taught and told because it would reveal a lot of facts (AFRICANS were here). How we are the superior beings, how we are the most powerful, the most intelligent. The proof is there. The truth is there, but they erased it, and unfortunately, most of us (black and brown) don't even believe it. Because we have been brainwashed and beaten down so much that we have no dignity and pride, it just cracks me up how all of these black people just love America, the USA… "What has America done for your black ass"? Answer me that because I know it hasn't done a fuckin thing for me.

THE DREAM

If we, as a black community, start thriving and building on our own, doing big things, great things, in and for our own selves, they will come and burn it down and destroy it. That's unfortunate, but it's facts! Black Wall Street was real!!

60TH BIRTHDAY

January 25th, 2022. I'm three weeks into the new year, so I must start writing again. I turned 60 on November 16th of last year. Thank God I made it. We're going into the third year of this covid-19 bullshit!!! So it's been a very rough two and a half years, but I'm a survivor, thank you, God. Unfortunately, I've

THE DREAM

lost several friends and a couple of family members to this crazy man-made, government-infested disease. I am not going to spend much time talking about that, but it can't be ignored because this is the world we live in today. It's really hard to find out what is real and what is not. It's really hard to believe what the people on the news are telling us. I'm so sick of the powers that be, lying to us and expecting us to take it with a grain of salt like we've been taking everything else from day one. There are millions of people who are getting vaccinated. I'm not one of them. I have come to the realization there's nobody on this planet that cares about me more than me, so I have to do what I need to do: protect myself, take care of myself, and navigate through this unfair, brutal, heinous world we live in. This pandemic is news, but it's just like everything else that we've been lied to and deceived about from the beginning of time. Well, enough of that. I'm here to tell my story, but that's just what type of environment we're living in in 2022.

Even though it's been very devastating and very difficult to adjust to the new normal, I really can't complain because I had a really good 2021. I reached the goals that I set …While I was a little shy of the exact goal, to be honest, I was still very pleased with the outcome. I had made a goal for 2022. I said I was going to go invest in the stock market, diversify my portfolio, and try to get my nest egg in order so if I make it into my mid-80s or later, I won't be one of those people that I look at all the time in dread… when I go to a restaurant or Walmart or anywhere in the mall, and I see these elderly people 75 and up still working. I always say God, please don't let that be me. Now, don't get me wrong, if I have a lot of energy and I'm bored I will take on a volunteer situation or a work situation just to keep me vibrant and alive. But I pray that I don't have to work at that age because I didn't plan well.

TRAVEL AGENT

This journey, this thing called life, which I am closer to the end, than the beginning or the middle of, I've come to terms with myself that my budgeting and money situation is not where it needs to be by any means. So that's what I'm focusing on. I'm investing in stocks I am trying to save to be a homeowner in the next year or two and I am trying to make my money make money for me.

    I have literally worked all my life. My first job was when I was 6 or 7 years old at the Grove Street Bakery. I was just reminiscing with my best friend Joy, telling her how I started working there, how he used to pay me in desserts, and I would run home with all my pastries and donuts for us to have for dessert after dinner. Every day, I would go after school and sweep up the floor and do whatever he told me to do, and I'd get my desserts and take them home. I felt like I was contributing to the household; it was a good feeling, and I always felt like I wanted to work if I liked what I did.

THE DREAM

Eventually, he would give me some change and desserts, and I was happy with both. From that day forward, I knew I liked working, and I knew I liked being rewarded for my work.

My DREAM, was to see the world. I knew I had to travel. Like I said before, I have had the traveling bug ever since my nana took us to different destinations as young kids. My first dream job was a travel agent. That was the best job ever, but of course, all good things come to an end. I worked for Liberty Travel, which was ten minutes from home up on the hill in a neighboring town. I was in my early twenties, and I was traveling all over the world. The ladies in the office had husbands and children, so they weren't eager to go anywhere for three or four days, but I was jumping on every trip that was available. I also had a great manager. Kathy Velez (R.I.P.) I also considered her a friend. She had a hustle mentality like I did. We had the number-one office in the region for quite a few years. There were six or seven agents. I was the only guy in the office for a while, and most of the ladies I would consider friends. Kathy & Liza were like Lucy and Ethel from the I Love Lucy show, funny and witty but worked really well together. Our secretary Rosie was my favorite. We share the same birthday. We started a week apart, and we just had a bond. She was old-school Italian and loved to cook, and she used to bring us the best Italian dishes ever!!!

Denise Rukaki was a cute blonde and was one of the top agents. She and Liza were very competitive. But Kathy, Liza, and I went on a lot of the travel agent meetings and dinners. You can win lots of prizes, family trips, and all kinds of exciting stuff. Like I said, that was one of the best jobs ever. But, once Kathy got promoted and brought in one of her girlfriends from another office to run our office, everything went downhill. This bitch June was probably a descendant of Hitler because that's how she ran the office. She was dumb as a stick and that's probably why she was so mean because she didn't want people to find out who she really was. Pathetic. Like I said, before Kathy left and got her promotion, we were number one in the region. That quickly digressed once Dodo brain came into the office. Of course, you know I don't bite my tongue, so I didn't take her shit. Instead of talking to me like a human being, she'd write me little notes and stick them on my computer screen.

So, I got fed up with June's bullshit. I called out sick, went to New York, and had an interview with Bahamas Express. I came to work the next day late, just to piss her off. Everybody else in the office knew my plan except June. I had told them I was leaving a week before because I knew I would kill her if I stayed. And she thought she fired me, but you can never outsmart me. You stupid bitch I got fired so I could collect unemployment. Seriously, she was dumb as a stick. She didn't know anything, but she had a brown noser in the office that did all her work and covered up her illiteracy. He really should have been the manager. She was so bad that nine people left that office the year she was there. She gave this young lady, Sally, who sat next to her, shingles because she was so stressed out (poor thing). A couple of years later, the ladies from the office decided to venture on their own, and they opened up a travel agency in Bloomfield, New

THE DREAM

Jersey. I worked there on a commission basis. It lasted a couple of years, but there was no competing with those big chains of travel agents.

GRASSROOTS

I saw one of my Grassroots kids, a full-grown adult, doing very well. I was in New Orleans at the Essence Festival about seven or eight years ago. He was working for Nephew Tommy from the (Steve Harvey Morning Show.) Unbeknownst to me. I was at the Convention Center going from booth to booth, and I saw my Nephew Tommy taking photos with everybody, but the line was long as hell, and lo and behold, there's Chuck. He sees me, I see him, and we embrace. "What's up? How are you feeling? What's going on? What are you doing here?" I asked him, and he asked me. We were really just ecstatic to see each other from the "Claire." He brought me to the front of the line and said to Nephew Tommy, "This is Maurice. He was my counselor when I was a kid in Grassroots." That touched my heart. "Hey man, Nephew Tommy," he said, grabbed and hugged me, and we took a nice picture together. That really made my day.

THE DREAM

The one thing I know for sure is that when you move through life doing the best you can and honoring yourself and GOD more times than not, your path is pretty solid. The way you move and the way you carry yourself, and respect yourself and others shines through. Now, don't get me wrong, of course, we all have bad days, and the sun's not always shining. But, when you have positive energy in your life and a good vibe on a continuous basis, your life reflects that. What bothers me and where I think there's a disconnect is in the black community. Especially when I hear, and I hear it a lot, unfortunately, "I'ma let God. It's in God's hands,", "Imma give it to God", "God find me a man', "God find me a woman" "God find me a job". God did say you can lean on him, but he didn't say bury him, suffocate his ass. DAMN. When God made us, he made us pretty well-equipped. God gave us most of the tools needed to work with and also what we needed to navigate through this thing called life. A lot of us get lost and take different paths, but there are lessons in everything we do. Good, bad, or indifferent. He said to come to him with all your problems and worries. But guess what? You have to put forth the effort as well. YOU have to take the first step. You have to have the attitude to overcome, to get what you want. You can't just say, "Oh, I want a husband or a wife. I want a job, a car, a house," and do nothing. So, just because you take a couple of seconds to pray, not really even praying, practically begging to GOD. So he's just supposed to stop, just for your lazy ass? I don't think so. That's not how life works!!! "I'mma leave it to God." Please. That's some lazy negro shit!! A lot of people are guilty of that, and you know who you are. And don't even get me started on religion and the church, especially the black church. That's another whole book! I'm sure I'll revisit that, but not right now.

DON

So I'm taking care of my ex Don. Things were going as planned. He was recovering from his hip surgery, but then another whole turn of events happened within the first two weeks I was there. I ended up caring for his boss as well because her caregiver just walked out. It worked to my benefit because I made good money, but it was a lot. So basically, it was the three of us quarantining in the house. Once in a while, people came by to visit to check on Don and Shelly. They also had a physical therapist coming two or three days a week to work on both of them. Dominic is a really cool brother. He knew what he was doing. He worked them really hard, but it was worth the pain because he had them whipped into shape.

I met Don in February 2011, we became fast friends, and we enjoyed each other's company. I was fresh out of a five-year relationship, so by no means did I want to jump into anything serious then. Don was four years my senior. A very handsome Big Brother, about

6'3 350. I felt bad because I always described him and compared him to a Ruben Studdard type when I was telling my sister about him. And I think that was an over-exaggeration for sure. He was never that big, plus he was much better looking. He lives in the D.C. area and is the VP of one of the top realtor agencies in the DC, so he does very well for himself. A beautiful home, cars, the whole nine. Our friendship/relationship happened very quickly, and as I said, we enjoyed each other's company. I lived in New Jersey. He lived in the DC area, but I was kind of going down there every weekend or every other weekend because I wasn't seeing or dating anyone, and I was focused on my work. Our first trip together was to Florida, I would say, about a month or two after we started becoming closer friends. At this point, we still hadn't been intimate, just hugging, kissing hello and goodbye, and stuff like that, but I knew I was starting to fall for him. Now, the thing is, over my lifetime, I've dated a lot of different people, races, ethnicities, men, women, etc. I've never been intimate with a large man like Don. But I knew I was falling for him and fast. I just had it in my head that I would cross that bridge when it happened.

Anyway, he planned this whole trip to Florida. He just asked me if I was available, and he took it from there. So, the night before, I took the Bolt Bus down from Newark Penn Station to Union Station, DC's bus terminal. It was like 15 bucks round trip. I stayed at his house in the guest room because we were leaving from Dulles Airport in the morning. The bus pulled into the station at 5:15 pm, and Don picked me up at 5:30. It was a smooth ride down. I was all excited. As soon as I stepped off the bus, I got a text from Don saying, "I'll be there in 10 minutes." I text him back, "Great, I just got off the bus. I'll see you soon." He pulled up in his Porsche SUV. I'm smiling from ear to ear as he opened the trunk I put my stuff in. Then, I jumped in the passenger seat, leaned over, and kissed him hello. "Hey you," I said, all giggly and excited. "What are you all excited about?" he asked as he was smiling at me. "Because I'm here with you, and we're going to Florida together tomorrow, that's why. Is that okay with you?" I asked as I reached for his hand to hold. I was just leaning back in the car seat, getting settled in. Don was driving, and I was just looking out the window. Then, I turned to him. "So, how was work?" I asked. "Good" he replied. "Same shit, different day," he added, and we both laughed.

I guess I dozed off. "Hey Maurice," Don called as he tapped my leg. "We're here," he said. "Unload everything because we're taking a car service in the morning. So just put your big suitcase and stuff by the door and all the rest of the stuff upstairs," he said. "Oh, okay, cool," I replied. I unloaded everything, put my suitcase by the door, and took my other stuff upstairs to the guest room. Then he asked me, "What do you want to do for dinner? Do you want to cook something? Do you want to order takeout or go out? Your call," he said. Well, I figured the least I could do was cook him a really nice home-cooked meal. After all, he was taking me to Florida for four days. So I went down and looked in the refrigerator, and I saw a nice piece of filet salmon that he had taken out of the freezer earlier. "Now, what kind of vegetables do we have in here?" I was saying to myself as I moved stuff around and looked. I decided to prepare blackened salmon, roasted Brussels sprouts, sweet potatoes, and maybe a side salad. He was in his office doing some stuff on the computer. I yelled out, "Dinner should be ready in about 45 minutes." "Sounds good," he replied. So I'm in there doing my thing, which is one of the things that I'm very good at. I can throw down in the kitchen. If I do, say so myself. I have fed thousands of folks, so my food speaks for itself.

"Come and get it. Dinner is served," I yelled out toward his office. "Okay, I'll be there in a minute," he answered. I put a little extra touch on it. I set the table really nicely, lit a few candles, used cloth napkins, and dimmed the lights a little bit. I had fixed our plates, so when he walked in, he was like, "Wow, looks good." I said "Sit, let's eat. Oh, I wasn't sure what you wanted to drink. Did you want unsweet tea or bottled water?" "I'll do water for right now, thanks," he said. I grabbed his water, we sat down and had a wonderful dinner. "Oh my God, that was delicious," Don said. "It was pretty good. I put my foots in it," and we laugh. "Hey, there's some sorbet in the freezer if you want a little dessert," he told me. "Thanks, maybe in a few," I said.

I got us a little dessert, went up to his room, and we watched TV for about an hour.

THE DREAM

"We got to be up and ready by 6 am, right?" I asked. "Yes, our flight is at 8:30," he replied. "Okay, I'm out. Bedtime for me," I told him as I leaned over and gave him a kiss on the lips. As I headed to the guest room, I called back, "I'll see you in the A.m." "Good night," Don called back. "And thanks again for the wonderful dinner," he added. "Sure thing. There's plenty where that came from. Night," I said as I was walking down the hallway.

At 5:05 a.m., I was up and full of anticipation with a big smile on my face. I heard movement in Don's room, so I guess he was getting dressed and everything. It was 5:50, and the driver was out front, so we took our stuff to the car, jumped in, and were on our way to Dulles Airport. As we were walking through the terminal, Don left to go use the restroom. So, I took that opportunity and called my friend Stretch in Florida to tell her that my new boo and I were going to be down there. Anyway, to my surprise, we get to the counter, well, I get to the counter, thinking that was where we checked in at. I saw Don walking past me, and I asked, "Where you going? Isn't this where we check in?" He ignored me, and the next thing I knew, we were checking in first class. "Well, you go, boi," I was thinking in my head. So far, so good. First class to Florida, so I can only wonder where we're staying.

THE DREAM

I slept most of the way in my nice wide leather cushion first-class seat. It was almost time to land, so of course, the loud ass intercom woke me up. "Ladies and gentlemen. We have twenty minutes before we land, so please put your tray tables up, put your seat into the upright position, fasten your seatbelts, and enjoy the rest of the flight until we land in sunny Florida," the flight attendant said. There was a car service waiting for us after we collected our bags, and now we were off to the hotel. We pulled up to this 5-star hotel (A TRUMP hotel). Well, this was before the asshole was president and before I knew he was batshit crazy. I wouldn't be found dead in one of his hotels now!!! Anyway, our room wasn't ready, so we just went to the pool. He got a drink, and I got a strawberry virgin colada. We just chilled until our room was ready.

I walked up to the front desk. "Hi, I'm just looking to see if we could check in now," I said to the nice-looking young lady standing there. "Sure, sir. What's the last name, please?" she asked. "It's Don Juan," I replied. "Yes, sir, you guys are all set. I apologize for the delay, and because of that, we upgraded you to a one-bedroom suite. I hope you find everything to your liking. If you need anything, please don't hesitate to give us a call," the young lady, Terry, said to me as she was handing me the keys to our suites. "Wow, thanks so much, Terry," I said with a big smile on my face.

We turned toward the elevator and went to the 35th floor. I'm in my head bugging. Four days in Florida (check) first class tickets (check) five-star hotel 35th floor (check.) We get to Room 3528, and I open the door to a nice-sized living room with a couch, a loveseat, and a beautiful ocean view with a sliding door to a balcony. There was also a round table with seating for four and nice pictures hanging on the walls. We walked into the bedroom, and there was a huge king-size bed with a sofa chair in the corner. A big 55" flat-screen television hung on the wall in front of it. The interior design was really well-thought-out and very nice. And there was a pretty big bathroom with a huge shower that could probably fit four people (check, check, check). Don's a keeper!!! He had a smile on his face, so I guess it was to his liking, and he is not an easy man to please. Quiet as it's kept, he had a little air about him, but that's also a part of him that I liked. I would put him in check once in a while. Sometimes, he'd have a condescending tone or a dismissive way about him. I would call him out at times or just tell him to get his damn head out of the clouds and get back to reality. He knew what I meant.

THE DREAM

Sometimes, we (individuals) do things on a daily basis, and we get comfortable in our own skin, and we may say things or do things that might not make other people around us feel so good. I don't think we realize it, but who knows, maybe we/he does realize it.

It's 89 degrees in sunny Florida, so we decided to go down to the beach for a while. I love the water. Don got his feet wet and then sat in his beach chair with his drink and chilled. He took a couple of pictures. I swam for a little while, and then we went up and had a beautiful early romantic dinner in the room. We got upstairs, and it was about 6:15 p.m., and I was ready to throw down because swimming makes you really hungry. I was looking over the menu, "Oh, I know what I want," I said to Don. "I'm going to have the crab cakes, asparagus tips, sweet potatoes, and a house salad." "Oh, that sounds good. I definitely want the crab cakes," Don said as he called down and placed our order. Within 30-35 minutes, our food was delivered. The waiter put our food on the table, "Can I get you guys anything else? "Antonio asked. "No, thanks. Antonio, have a good evening," I said as he took his cart out the door. Don handed him a generous gratuity as he walked out. "Let's eat," I said. "Oh, this looks good," Don said as he was uncovering his food. He ended up getting two crab cakes, garlic mashed potatoes, and string beans. We didn't talk much over dinner because I was so busy stuffing my face. It was very tasty, and to top it off, we shared a piece of chocolate cake and a piece of carrot cake.

After dinner, we sat around on the couch and watched TV. We were watching this really good movie, which the name slips my mind. A commercial came on. Don turns to me and says, "I'm going to get in bed. I can't keep my eyes open." I looked at him, kind of baffled, only because the movie was ending in about 15 minutes, and it was really intense. A lot was going on, and we were getting ready to find out the answer and the conclusion. "It's over in

THE DREAM

another fifteen minutes. You don't want to see the ending?" I asked, in excitement and disbelief. "No, you go ahead. Good night," he replied. "Good night. I'll be in there soon," I said back.

Now remember, there's only one bed, and this will be our first time in the same bed together except for when we were watching TV back at his house, but we never slept in the same bed. So now I'm thinking to myself, is this going to be the night that we consummate our relationship? What do I say? What do I do? All this swirling in my head, all these things… what ifs, what ifs.

THE DREAM

Finally, I go into the bedroom, and to my surprise, he's all the way on the far end of the bed, almost hugging the wall. So now I'm thinking, okay, once I get in the bed then maybe he'll roll over and make his move. I'm laying there still a little tense because I don't know how to respond if he happens to come on to me. At this point, I know I really like him, but I don't want to make the first move. I still don't know about lovemaking because of his size. It was just a lot of stuff going on in my head. Next thing I knew, it was 7 in the morning, and nothing happened. When I looked, he was still way over there. I was about to get up and go pee as he was turning over, "Good morning," he said. "Good morning," I replied. As I was walking to the bathroom, I said, "So you slept like a baby." "I sure did. I was worn out from the sun, I guess," he replied.

"So, what do you feel like doing today?" I asked. "Doesn't matter to me. Let's play it by ear. We can do the pool or the beach or both," he said. We decided to have a little breakfast, and then we would figure out what we were going to do. Eventually, we decided to go down to the pool for a little while. Then Don mentioned that he wanted to go walk on Lincoln Road and do some shopping. So after I finished playing in the pool for about an hour, we decided to go to Lincoln Road to have some lunch and do a little shopping.

Now, personally, I'm not a shopper. I don't like it. But Don, on the other hand, could shop all day. There's this restaurant that I go to every time I'm in Miami on Lincoln Road. It's called Nexxt. They have great calamari and a lot of other good stuff so we ate there. We finished our lunch, and we agreed that we'd go shopping for a little bit and then get dessert somewhere else. I was hoping and praying that the shopping situation wouldn't take long because, as I said, I didn't like it. We walked in and out of a few stores, and I think that is what it is. It's the air conditioning that gets me. It's nice and sunny outdoors, and then you go into these freezing air-conditioned stores. I just can't stand the cold, and the abrupt change really messes with my body, so I opted to wait outside the last couple of stores that he went into.

He walked into the Swatch watch store, then he came right back out and said, "Come here for a second. I want you to look at this watch." I hemmed and hawed, and eventually, I ended up giving in. "It's freezing in here. I don't want to see no watches anyway," I exclaimed. He asked me if I liked any watches, and I pointed to the first two I saw and ran out of the store. I'm serious. It was like icicles in there to me. About four or five minutes later, he walked out of the store and handed me a Swatch bag. "Here. You're like an old lady. It's not even that cold in there," he said, teasing me. I took the bag, looked in it, opened it up, and it was a rose-colored watch. "Oh my GOD, thank you! I didn't want a watch. I don't need a watch," I protested. "Well, you got it now, so shut up and enjoy it," he chided back. "Okay, thanks," I said as I was trying to put on my new pretty rose-colored watch with encrusted diamonds on the face.

Now I'm walking down Lincoln Road, grinning from ear to ear with my new watch on my wrist. I saw an ice cream spot, so I said, "Hey, let's go in here and see if they have sorbet." "Hmm, that looks good," Don said as he pointed to the raspberry mango swirl. He said to the guy, "I'll have a double scoop of that, please." "What can I get for you, sir?" the gentleman asked me. "Oh, I'll do one scoop of the strawberry and one scoop of the lemon sorbet, please. Thank you," I replied.

We're just walking down Lincoln Road enjoying our sorbet, and of course, I'm in my head again. Great lunch (check), new Swatch watch (check), two scoops of sorbet (check) …Don's definitely a keeper (check). We got back to the hotel at about 4:30 ish, and I decided that I was going to take a nap and just chill until dinner time. So, I walked into the bedroom and laid across the bed. Don turned on the TV in the living room area and looked into the bedroom. He called out, "Enjoy your nap. I'm going to watch TV for a little while."

"Okay, cool," I replied and drifted off to La La Land. We dated for 11 months.

ALBUM

On Monday, August 15th, 2022, I accomplished another thing on my bucket list. I recorded two songs in a real recording studio in Nashville, Tennessee. It was a fun experience, and the two songs came out pretty good. I don't have the voice that I used to have, but I can still hold a note. The first was "Love On a Two-way

Street" by The Moments. The second was "Inseparable" by Natalie Cole. I'm glad I got the opportunity and the experience. I wasn't nervous actually, but when I listened back to the CD, I wish

I would have done it over again. But it's a done deal. It's okay. Like I said, I was grateful for the experience. I purchased a 10" x 10" gold record frame with the name of the song that I sang and two pictures of me singing so I'll have those memories.

Flash forward to Friday, September 23, 2022. It was my friend JD's birthday. His boo Tony was throwing him a surprise dinner party and invited me over to celebrate with them. JD and I have been friends for probably 25 years or more, and we used to hang out with a group of people. That was lots of fun, but I hadn't been around these people in years because one of the guys who used to throw really good parties stopped speaking to me about 15 years ago. To this day, I have no clue why. I only bring this to the forefront because I just thought it was a petty situation. A lot of people around me who were supposed to be my friends knew why he wasn't speaking to me and didn't say anything. He never said anything either, so my attitude was I can give a shit. I'm a grown man. We could have had a grown-man conversation if I did anything to hurt this person, or we could have talked out the misunderstanding. But if he chooses not to speak, then I have no problem with it. I don't have time for petty bullshit. What I know for sure is that life is very short. So, the time I have left on this Earth, I want it to be peaceful, zen, and happy.

That's how I'm living these days. So, I went to the party. I met a couple of nice people that I never saw before, and I saw some old faces, and it was really nice and actually, the two people that I hadn't seen or spoken to were there. I said hello. They probably felt like I was being shady and I can't tell them how to feel, but what I do know is that I'm not a fake person, so I was not about to act all happy, giddy, huggy, and kissy and shit. I don't do that. I spoke, and that was it. I continue to mingle and have fun with other people. Now, if I were to see that couple again, maybe we could have that conversation. But the fun part about being there for me was this young lady named Denna Steel. She's a singer, and she serenaded JD with a "Happy Birthday" song. I said, "Oh shit, she has some pipes." Anyway, I saw her coming into the kitchen, "Excuse me, are you a singer?" I asked. "Yes, I am," she replied. "I knew it. When you were singing Happy Birthday to JD? I was enjoying your voice," I explained. She smiled. As we walked together toward the empty living room, I added, "I want to ask you a question. I just recorded a song, and if you could be so kind as to listen to it and critique it for me, I would appreciate it." "Sure, no problem," she said. So, I played my recording of "Inseparable" by Natalie Cole, who I love. She said to me, "Well, you can definitely sing." We listened to it again, and then she said, "See, this is where I could tell you were a little nervous, but otherwise, really nice voice." Two other people came into our little circle and listened to my song. This other guy named Christian was also into singing, so we listened to his song/music and critiqued it, and then they listened to my singing and critiqued it. So, we all

THE DREAM

exchanged numbers and promised to keep in touch, so that was really fun.

YVETTE

Yvette and I have known each other for over 50 years. We've had a special relationship on and off for many years. She lives in the Maryland area, and I visit her a few times a year. It's pretty routine. We have dinner, hang out, laugh, sing, and watch TV. Sometimes we're intimate, but lately or the last two times, it's stopped at the watching TV part. I didn't push, I didn't pursue, I didn't try, but I slept on the couch, and I was fine with that. This year, 2023, I believe that things should happen organically, and if they don't, then I'm okay with the outcome. I spoke to Yvette probably four or five years ago about us growing old together, looking out and taking care of one another if we didn't have a significant other. It was nothing deep, nothing heavy. I put it out there, and she said it was something to think about. but what I realized is that she's where she's at, and she's going to be there probably for the rest of her life because she has some issues with traveling. She hasn't left Maryland in years and probably

THE DREAM

has no intentions of doing so. I just have to

love her from a distance because I hate the cold,

and I have no intentions of living in Maryland.

I'll just visit in the spring and summer months.

2023

2023 is the year for me to purge. To let go of things that don't bring me joy, to end friendships that are holding me back, weighing me down. I came into this world alone, and I'm probably going to leave it alone, and I'm good with that. I'm a people person, but I'm not a bullshiter, and I don't like bullshit. And the older

I get, the less tolerant I am of people and their bullshit. Their selfishness, their self-centeredness. I'm a giver and a good man, and I have good intentions, but I will not tolerate disrespect or ignorance. I'm just done with it all. I like to laugh, and I like to have a good time. I like Good Vibes and Good Vibrations. If you're with me, then we'll be vibing. If you're not, then have a nice life. I don't wish any malice or harm to anyone; I just can't be a part of what you've got going on. If it's not joy, peace, and Souuul trainnnn…just kidding. Take a joke. No, seriously, I don't have time for the crap that a lot of human beings are putting out there. I have an agenda. I have A Dream, and my dream is to

THE DREAM

enjoy life, vacation on different continents every year, laugh, love, eat, sing, dance, relax, and chill till the end of my time… until then, I'll see you on the other side.

JACKSONVILLE

I'm in Jacksonville, Florida, working, getting some sun, and visiting my sister. One of my clients that I see here is a really cool guy. I think I've been massaging for about two years now and I kind of got a crush on him. He knows it now because I kind of told him. With his clothes on, he's probably a six, but undressed, I could really appreciate his physique. So, he's more like a nine. Not real muscular, has a medium frame, built, but he has the perfect ass. A nice dick and ball sack too.

So we were just chatting it up, and he has this sexy baritone voice that takes me to another place as well. I was telling him about shit that was going on with me, and we were laughing at stuff, and then he was like, "You should write a book." I replied back, "I am." So, you made the book, fantasy man. Like I said, I've been on this dude for about two years. When he first walked into the room, I introduced myself and told him he could put his stuff in the chair right there, and to lay face down on the table. When I looked at him lying on my table, I realized his ass was perfect. It was my first time massaging him, so I knew I had to be professional and play it cool. So I started to massage him, but I also started to fantasize about his ass. "Okay man, get a grip. You don't know what this guy's into. You can't think sexual thoughts," I'm saying to myself. At this point, I could feel my erection coming on, but I had on my underwear because he was just getting a basic massage. But when I started working on his glutes, the only thing I could think about was just sticking my tongue between his legs and having my way with him.

But I kept my composure and made it through. But, when I asked him to turn over, his dick was hard, and it was very attractive. So then, I felt the bulge in my pants, but I still didn't make a move because he was new.

So, over time, we got more comfortable with each other, and I kind of told him that I fantasized about his ass and that I was attracted to him and that I wanted us to have a happy ending together or something in that nature it still hasn't taken place in real time but a lot of things have happened in my mind, so that's why he's my fantasy man.

Now, I'm all excited and jittery because I know Fantasy Man has an appointment at

8:30 this evening. My phone dings I have a text message. It's 8:25. "Hey man, I'm here," the message reads. "Come on in. I'm in room 103," I tell him. Knock knock. I open the door. "Hey, man. How you doing? Come on in," I say. "I'm well. What's good?" he replies. "You can put your stuff in the chair there and then jump on the table, and let's get started." "Oh man, I'm so glad you're in town. I really need this. I've been stressed out," he said to me. "Don't worry, I got you," I said as he laid down on my table. I had Luther Vandross playing in the background "Here and Now."

I was staring at his ass, saying to myself, "Damn, what I would do to that…hmmm

hmmm. Okay, calm down. Do your job and stay in your zone. Act professional." Luther's singing his heart out. I was massaging my fantasy man, thinking all types of good, dirty thoughts. He was being really inquisitive, asking me different things, and I was telling him different stories, and we were cracking up. As I was speaking, I was massaging his ass. We were laughing, and I was lingering, feeling his ass. So, I slipped a finger in, and he didn't reject it. But then, I was nervous because I was wondering if I should go a step further and see what happened or do I stop and continue to be professional because I didn't want to lose him as a client. Well, of course, my libido took over, and I was in my head thinking, "Oh he wants me because I stuck a finger in his ass." So, I took my shot. I was massaging his ass using my different techniques and strokes, then I came around between his legs caressing his balls and insert a finger into his warm juicy and inviting hole, "How does that feel? You good?" I asked. "I'm good man. You always make me feel good", he replied. "Oh shit, is that a green light? Should I try more?" I'm asking in my head. A thousand things were spinning around in there. "I'm going for it," I said to myself.

I started massaging his thighs and down to his calves, then one long stroke up to his cheeks and slid my fingers between his legs down to his calves back up to his cheeks and inserted a finger again, this time he moaned in ecstasy. "Ohh shitttt, dat feels nice," he moaned. So, I continue massaging. Now, at this point, my dick is rock-hard, so I removed my briefs. I was still not 100% sure where this was going, but I hoped it was going in my favor. From the signs that I was getting, it seemed to be happening. I was at the end of the table where his feet were, and his legs were apart, so I decided to mount the table stroking him from his ankles upwards towards his warm moist asshole. My adrenaline was at 100, so there was no turning back. I stuck my hand between his cheeks to feel the pucker of his asshole. It was very warm and inviting, so I started kissing his inner thighs, and then I got to the bullseye. I started to lick and caress it, and his hips started to gyrate. He moaned out in ecstasy, "Oh man, you driving me crazy. This shit feels so good," he said and a sexy baritone voice. So, I knew it was on then. I started tossing his salad like it was no tomorrow. The massage had ended, and the sex had begun... "Hey man. Let's go over to the bed. I want you to enjoy every inch of me," I said. He walked over to the bed and laid down on his stomach. I'm like, oh shit, this is really about to go down. The lube and condoms were right on the nightstand, but I needed a little more foreplay just to get him wet and ready. I lay on top of him, kissing on his back, working my way down to his butt, and then going to town on dat perfect ass of his…. Fantasy man no more. That shit was real…real good!!! Thanks, sexy.

NEW ORLEANS

I'm headed to Birmingham, Alabama today. I hope business picks up. After that, I'll be going to one of my favorite cities, New Orleans, Louisiana. Great food, great people, and a real partying city, even though I don't party anymore. But my favorite is the Harrah's Casino. Oh yes, one of my best casino stories

THE DREAM

happened at Harrah's in New Orleans in 2016. I won $35,000 in three or four minutes in the poker room. I walked into the poker room, looking for a 4/8 table. Both tables were full, but there was a waiting table with three people there. I made the fourth person. About a minute after I sat down, three people from the playing table got up. Well, this old white guy named Lou (R.l.P) said, "Oh, Bob is over there. I don't want to play with him." "Hey Lou, can I go in your spot," I said excitedly. "Sure, go ahead. I don't give a crap. I'll wait for the next table," he says. I walked over to the table, and there was a guy standing in between two seats, so I said to him, "What seat do you want, sir?

Seat 4 or Seat 5?" He leaned towards seat four and then looked at seat five, then he said, "Okay, you go to seat four, and I'll sit in 5." Then this other guy said, "Come on. Sit down. Let's hit that bad beat." Now, mind you, the "bad beat" jackpot is over $270,000.

We sat down, and the dealer dealt out the first hand…nothing. He dealt the second hand, and I got an ace of clubs and a three of clubs. The flop was a two of clubs, a four of clubs, and an ace of hearts. The turn card was an ace of diamonds. I had a straight flush draw in clubs. The only thing I needed was a five of clubs, and it was the last card, which is the river. He turned it over to reveal a five of clubs, so I knew I was winning this hand. Now, mind you, I was betting the whole time because I just needed that five of clubs to win. There was like $300 in the pot, and when I saw the five clubs, I knew it was mine! But I had no idea that I was winning the jackpot!!! Everybody else folds their hand except the lady in seat six. When I bet $16, she saw the bet. The dealer says to show your hand. I turn over my straight flush, and she turns over quad aces... everybody starts screaming, and I was very happy because I had just won a $300 pot. Then the lady looked at me and said, "No we, you hit the bad beat, the jackpot!!! It didn't sink in at that second, and I was like, "What? What happened?" "We hit the bad beat!" everyone said all together. So I sat in my seat very excited, still not comprehending, but I knew I won a lot of money and then they told me how much I won. The lady got $70,000, I got $35,000, and the table got $5,000 each. It was a good day at Harrah's Casino.

With all the commotion and everything, everybody was looking through the glass partition, so people knew that something exciting was happening, and I was there with my friend Dennie. She came running in with these two other girls that I had never seen before pointing at me, so I mouthed to her that I had won some money, but I told her "Get out of here," because I didn't know who those people were that she was with. I passed off some cash, and I was very excited. I didn't tell anybody at home that I won, but I gave out a little money to my nephews and their families. I gave Dennie a couple hundred dollars. The dealer got a thousand, and a couple of dealers that I liked got 100. One of the best trips ever!!! When I got back home, I went and bought a 2012 White Altima in cash. I put the rest of the cash in the bank. In hindsight, I wish I had thought more about owning some land or a house or considering generational wealth and owning property; $27,000 would have been a nice down payment on a house. I'm single. Free. No kids, so my mindset wasn't there yet. Over

THE DREAM

the years, I've been in a whole new headspace. I'm trying to look towards the future, trying to get my ducks in a row and get that nest egg together. I was trying to purchase a piece of property before my 60th so I could have a big birthday bash in my own backyard. Because of Covid, we're still in the pandemic stages. I wanted everybody to feel safe, but it didn't come to fruition, but it's still not out of reach. Hopefully, by the end of 2023, I'll have something to call my own. Even though the buyer's market is a little crazy right now, I need to do it soon.

NICKI

I'm in Dallas, Texas, now getting ready to head to Houston. Business wasn't great, but a dear friend of mine, Nicki, lives here. I meant Nicki about six years ago at the American Black Film Festival down in Miami Beach. I was walking in the Loews Hotel, which was the host Hotel. I was just cruising through, seeing who I could see. There was nice music playing in the background and a very spacious bar area. There was a lounge area beyond that, which had tables and chairs for dining. A real nice setup. The vibe was good, and I was in there to see what stars I could spot and get some pics with.

I stood at the bar, and I ordered water with lemon, just checking out the scene. Right behind the bar, I heard lots of laughter and cracking up, so I walked that way to see what I could see. It was Tami Roman, Lisa Wu, and a couple of other young ladies in the area. So, of course, I'm ready to meet Tammy and Lisa Wu. Tammy has been on quite a few shows, but I know her from the Basketball Wives, and Lisa

Wu is from the Atlanta Housewives franchise. So I'm kind of just lingering in the area, and I make eye contact with Tammy, who is quite attractive in person. I kind of mouth hello, and she smiled back. So, at that moment, I decided to go ask if I could take a pic with her. "Hey Tammy, I'm a fan. Would it be possible to get a quick pic?" I asked. "Sure," she replied. So, as we were taking a selfie, I asked her if she thought Lisa would mind taking one with me as well, "I'm sure she wouldn't," she replied. "Hey Lisa," Tammy yelled. "Come take a picture with this brother. He wants to get a selfie with you." Lisa replied, "Absolutely." Once she got up to walk over toward me, I could tell she was feeling kind of good because she lost her footing.

Anyway, that kind of turned into a whole photoshoot with the ladies. I was taking pictures for them, and they were taking pictures with me. It was nice. They were really cool people, but they were enjoying their drinks. I said my thank yous, told them I'd catch them later, and continued to walk towards the bar. And that Lisa Wu, with her fine ass. She was being a little flirty.

So I approached the bar and just scoped out everybody, and I noticed these two young ladies sitting across on the other end. I walked over, introduced myself, and handed them my business card. "Good evening, ladies. How you doing?" I asked. "I'm Maurice." "Hey, Maurice, I'm Nikki, and this is Allison," the one girl replied. "Nice to meet you both," I said back. Now, Nikki caught my eye before I walked over to introduce myself. I watched them from afar. Nikki has medium brown skin, a beautiful smile, very nice dreads, and was giving cleavage for days. Allison is a nice-looking woman. She has light brown skin with a short crop haircut. So once I approached the ladies and had a full view, I realized Nikki was tall and curvy in all the right places. Like I said, Allison was a good-looking woman, but I wasn't attracted to her. Later on, I found out she was a singer, and she was going to be performing right there in the lounge. So we were just hanging out and having light conversations, and then it was time for Allison to perform. So, I sat down next to Nikki. The MC was on the mic, and he said, "Without further ado, and for your listening pleasure, please put your hands together for Miss Allison Bradshaw." The crowd clapped, and Nikki and I sat at the bar. Nikki yells out, "You go, girl!" and gives Allison the thumbs up. We were just sitting there enjoying Allison's sultry voice as she sang one of her original songs. She has a real sweet voice. "Ya girl can really blow. Very nice," I said to Nikki.

THE DREAM

Allison performed a 20-minute set, and Nikki and I were just getting to know each other and just talking in general. They're both from Jacksonville, Florida, and Allison had a steady gig at a blues lounge there, and she invited me to come check it out. I was telling them that my sister lives in Jacksonville, and I go there twice a year. "So, next time I'm in the area, I'll definitely check you out," I said to Allison. I bought a round of drinks, and right after they finished them, Nikki said to me, "So listen, Mr. Maurice. It's 1:15 in the morning. We're going to call it a night. It was great meeting you." "Great meeting you ladies as well," I replied. "Well, You have my card. I'll be hanging out at the pool tomorrow if y'all want to connect there," I said. "Oh, okay, cool, let's meet up tomorrow sometime. I'll call you," Nikki replied. "Looking forward to it. Y'all be safe. Take care," I said as the elevator door closed.

I got to the pool about 10:30 am, and I saved four chairs. As I was getting ready to take a dip in the pool, my phone rang. It's Nikki. "Hello," I answer. "Hey Maurice, it's Nikki," she replied. "Hey, Ms. Nikki. Are y'all gonna come and chill by the pool and hang out for a little while?" I asked. She replied, "Well, I'll be there in about ten minutes, but Allison has some things to do, so she might meet us later."

"Okay, cool," I said,

"So listen. When you walk down, look to your right, I'm in the third row over. You'll see four empty chairs and my black book bag sitting on the chair. I'll probably be in the pool because it's hot as fish grease out here all ready." She laughed. "Okay, see ya in a few," she said. I put my phone down and ran and jumped in the pool.

    I was swimming in the pool, just playing around, chilling, and waiting for Nicki to show up. I happened to look up, and she was coming down, walking towards the pool. "Hey Nikki, over here!" I shouted. She saw me, and I pointed in the direction of where I had my stuff. I got out of the pool and walked over to greet her. "Hey, what's going on?" I said as I gave her a hug. "Hey, Maurice. You go boi with your red trunks on…giving us body," she said, making me blush a little bit. I just smiled. "Hey, you going to get in the water, Nikki?" I asked. "No, you go ahead. I'm not really a water person. I might come and get my feet wet. You go ahead and have fun," she said, "Okay. I'll come check on you in a few," I replied. "Cool, I'll be right here checking my emails, on the phone, or reading a couple of my magazines chillin'," she said. I was off and headed back to the pool; it was hot as hell out there, but I love the water. I can swim all day. "What a life," I said to myself.

I was in Miami Beach, at the Black Film Festival, having a grand old time making shit happen, meeting real cool people. The whole vibe was just on point so far. I met a couple of T.V. Personalities, Roland Martin and Tom Joyner. Sherri Shepherd, my boi Darren Hansen, a celebrity, who I've met back in New Jersey a couple of times. Real cool brother and a damn good actor. Well, I will be here for another four days. No telling who I might run into. So far, so good. There was a Shaft III premiere that I definitely wanted to check out because I definitely wanted to meet Samuel L

Jackson, Richard Roundtree, Jessie T. Usher. I purchased a Shaft t-shirt, and I got Richard Roundtree and Samuel Jackson to sign it, so I was very grateful for that. Then I got the pleasure of meeting Master P., his son Romeo and Brois Kodjoe, and his fine wife Nicole Ari Parker. Now, that's the ultimate threesome. A whole slew of other folks that were in the movie game. The next day, I went to meet the crew from 50 Cent's hit Series on Starz Network, Ghost... I had the pleasure of meeting Omari Hardwick, Larenz Tate, Lahmard J. Tate, and LaLa Anthony.

GOALS

This journey, this thing called life, which I am closer to the end than the beginning or the middle of, I've come to terms with myself that my budgeting and money situation is not where it needs to be by any means. So that's what I'm focusing on. I'm investing in stocks I am trying to save to be a homeowner in the next year or two, and I am trying to make my money make money for me.

Now, I've lived, trust me, a pretty lavish lifestyle on a poor man's budget, but somehow, I've made it work. I know millionaires and billionaires who haven't seen or done some of the things I've managed to do and the places I've had the pleasure of visiting. A lot of the money-chasing guys are so dedicated to chasing the money they don't have time to vacation, enjoy the fruits of their labor, jump on the jet, take a cruise to relax. And enjoy life. Chasing that money is a full-time job, and most people are doing doubles and triple shifts. I just learned early in life that money wasn't the end or be all.

THE DREAM

You definitely need it; it's a good thing to have, but it doesn't run my life. I told my mother when I was just a young boy that I was going to see the world with a quarter in my pocket. And I'm still on that journey. There are seven continents. I've been on four. Asia and South America are next on my list.

Before this crazy Covid pandemic, my goal was to go to an African country every year. That crap really put a thorn in my side because I haven't traveled abroad in three years. So I stayed in the States, but I've driven from Boston down to Miami at least three or four times, and I've been to Hawaii over a dozen times. I have been out to California L.A, eight times, San Fran 5 times, and Palm Springs at least 9 nine times. But I'm still young enough, adventurous enough, and hopefully have the budget to fulfill that Journey. Two acquaintances of mine had mentioned retiring to Portugal. That's another spot that I have to explore. I've been to Australia. I had the pleasure of going to Sydney and Melbourne. Hopefully, I can do Australia again. I've been to Africa 4 different times. I've visited West Africa, Accra, North Africa, Morocco, Casablanca, Marrakesh, South Africa, Cape Town, and Johannesburg, one of my most favorite places. I've been throughout Europe, but there are some spots I still need to hit. I've been to

THE DREAM

London four times, Paris six times, Switzerland four times, Germany, Belgium, Austria, Amsterdam, Florence, Naples, Monaco, and Barcelona. So, my International game is pretty extensive. And I'm telling anyone who is reading this book that you don't have to have a lot of money to see the world. You just have to have your priorities and goals in order and put forth the effort to make them come to fruition. While everybody was bragging about all the money they were making, I was cruising, flying, eating, drinking, and living the life of the Rich and Famous, but I wasn't rich or famous. I just knew what I wanted to do and did it!!

EXPECTATIONS

Expectations. It is something that we want or something that we're looking forward to. But over my years of experience in this thing called life, my expectations are very small and limited when it comes to the human species. I realize that life takes us through many stages and phases, but the one thing I learned about myself is that I'm pretty loyal. And respect and loyalty sit pretty high on my expectation list. Or at least it did.

A lot of people are into zodiac signs. I was never one who was really into it, but I will say this about myself: I am a Scorpio. I am loyal, but if you cross me, you will get stung! I believe I probably have had three physical altercations in my life. Seriously, I'm a very non-violent person. This probably stems from my father being so abusive to my mother, and I just didn't understand the purpose of it.

Now, in my mind, I've killed millions of people, but I always ask God for forgiveness and take it back. But physically, I'm not a violent person. And in this stage of the game, I'm not fighting a damn soul. I might shoot or cut a Nigger, but I'm not fighting nobody. I can usually talk or walk my way out of any situation, but if somebody puts hands on me, then that's another thing, but that hasn't happened over my lifetime.

But as far as I can remember, my way of thinking or my motto was always: I like most people until they gave me a reason not to. In my teenage years, I had my crew that I hung around with, but I was pretty much a jack-of-all-trades when it came to relationships. I can fit in or get along with almost anybody I knew. Literally all types of characters. The nerds, the cool people, the violent people. I literally know people who murdered people. I think I have known about four murderers in my lifetime, maybe more if I think hard. But my whole point is this: throughout your lifetime, you become friends with different people in different stages, and the word "friend" now today in 2022 is a term that is used very loosely. I have made a vow to GOD, probably about seven or eight years ago, that I was good with him and me (GOD) because most people are unreliable, and thank God that I never got into a situation where I really needed to count on anybody except my mother and Nana.

THE DREAM

I do a lot of my critical thinking between four and six in the morning, and I always think of scenarios like getting stuck on the road, getting locked up, or getting into some kind of heinous crime or something. I then thought about who I could call at five in the morning and say come bail me out, come pick me up, help me. I need $10,000 for bond. The real truth was probably nobody. But I did have some names in mind: Glen, Renee, Brad, and Missy. Realistically these people don't owe me a damn thing, but the hope is that I can rely on people that say they care about me and vice versa. But, my expectations of people that I care about, trust and love are just that…an expectation. I hope that they will come through for me, but they're not obligated to. And, a large percentage of the time, when you expect someone to come through, it's a letdown. I'm praying I never get into a situation where I would need to count on anyone. But the hope is that they will come through. However, from my experience, I wouldn't count on it.

The reality is people have their own lives, their own situations, and their own shit that they're going through. At the end of the day, I trust myself and God to get me through any situation that I'm in. The real funny thing is that most people are just so busy some people can't even answer the phone, return a phone call, or respond to a text, so do we really want to rely on that individual? That's how busy they think their lives are. It just baffles me, but that's why I've come to the conclusion that if I don't have any expectations, then I would never be let down or disappointed. And I'm ok with that. I'm at that stage now. Again, I'm not taking anything away from any of these people that I just named; I'm just stating facts. I never got into a situation where I would need to depend on any of these people solely, and I'm grateful for that.

One thing Covid has taught me was patience, to be still, and to really reflect on my life. To re-evaluate what I believe in, and who

THE DREAM

or what I could count on or trust. What I look forward to. I believe in myself wholeheartedly. I believe in my higher power(GOD), and I'm good with that. Again, nobody in this world owes me a damn thing, and I definitely don't owe anybody anything. I just know that throughout my relationships, familyships, friendships, and all the ships that there are, I've been a loyal and a good person to everybody.

All relationships have ebbs and flows; they're never really 50/50, and I understand that. But I've been let down and disappointed with a lot of people, so I just know that I'm good with believing in myself and trusting in myself and my higher power. I still love the thought of friendships. And being around others and enjoying people's company, but I just don't expect anything from anybody. I live my life on my terms, and I just try not to think about what I expect from anyone because then I won't be disappointed. I travel all over the country, and when the covid pandemic came out, the first thing I thought about was my "friends" and "family." I mean, I'm watching the TV and hear that hundreds of thousands of people are dropping dead, so naturally, my response was to reach out to people from New Jersey. I'm from New Jersey; that was my base, and it was really disappointing to find out that I practically had to beg people to respond to a text because I was reaching out to them to find out if they were breathing and still alive.

It was an eye-opener. I was just really taken aback because I know if I got a text that said, "Hey, hoping this text finds you healthy and well and I'm thinking about you, please let me know that you're okay," it would be a natural instinct for me to reach out. If I'm fine and well, respond to this text. There were quite a few people that didn't respond for quite a few days. Then, I would reach out again because now I'm worried. But no, they didn't think that that warranted a response. Especially when people were dying by the second because they

THE DREAM

were so inundated with their own selfish bull shit ass lives that it didn't mean a thing to them.

Listen, I grew up very fast, and again, I like most people until they give me a reason not to. I have 61 years in this life, and many people have given me that reason. And just because I don't deal with them or we're not friends. I wish them well in their journey and in their life. I just choose not to be a part of it. I forgive and keep moving on. I don't hold grudges. People do to you what you allow them to do, and I just don't allow myself to keep getting disappointed or hurt by selfishness.

THE DREAM

When I see people I haven't seen in a long time, say at a class reunion or something like that, they say, "Oh Maurice, you haven't changed. You're so funny; you're crazy." That part is true, but actually, I have changed… I've evolved in a lot of ways. I'm like a sponge. I'm always growing, I'm always trying to learn, and I'm always listening and watching. Every day, I'm learning something new. There's always a teachable moment in my life. I can't stay stagnant or comfortable in any particular situation, and I find a lot of people that I associate with have done that. I'm not judging; I'm just observing and making a statement. You do what's best for you and your life, and imma continue to do what's best for me and mine. And if you're on this journey with me, then great. If you're not, I wish you well.

I'm just thinking I received a phone call yesterday from Don, an ex of mine. But that triggered a thought in my head about people and my expectations. But I have to realize that I shouldn't expect anything from anybody because, most of the time, it brings disappointment. So I guess if I just meet people where they're at and just deal with them on a surface level and not expect or attempt to believe. They owe me anything because they really don't. Then I just think I'll be in a better place. No one owes me anything except respect and accountability. I won't look for anything more. I'm 61 now, and I don't need new friends. And the acquaintances that I have, I can take them or leave them. I guess it's sad to say, but it's true. The path that I'm taking, I'm trying to be the best me that I can be and when I look back at the people that I surround myself with, I'm really not seeing any kind of growth. I'm not judging; it's just an observation, and unfortunately, I think I'm over it. I need to surround myself with people who stimulate my mind and people who can have in-depth conversations about life and things with substance. What's that old saying, "If you're the smartest person in the room, you need new friends." Well, that's what I've been feeling over the last couple of years.

STICKING TOGETHER

The one thing I could give white people credit for is that they all stick together no matter what! You see what's happening right now in 2022. But we can't get shit together on our own, and it's a sad, sad time. We have no leaders. We have nobody we can trust because all these coons out here, they act like they're for us and don't give a shit about us! I still say if we had MEN like the honorable Louis Farrakhan, Dr. Claude Anderson, Dr. Umar Johnson, Professor Griff, Kyrie, Nick Cannon, Black men with knowledge and some balls to stand up and tell the truth, speak the truth, we might have a fighting chance, but I don't know why they all can't get together and come to an understanding of one accord. Once they killed Martin Luther King and Malcolm X and all the other people that we had as leaders. There hasn't been any like it since, a shame, I say.

To me, the whole franchise of sports NFL, NBA, etc., can all kick rocks because those punk-ass rich, ignorant Negroes if they only had the sense that God gave them. When Kaepernick took that knee and all those Slaving/Coons scared to lose a bag, Negroes did not stand with him. I was done. That would have changed the whole trajectory of our people. That would have been one of the biggest stances that had ever taken place in the world. Think about it. Follow me for a second …I don't know all the stats, but I'm going to take a guess: in the sports world, I would think at least eighty percent or more black men and women or people of color dominate the league. If they would have taken a knee and stood in solidarity with Kaepernick, there would have been so much Black Power, so much black

Pride, and so much FREEDOM!!! But you enslaved rich Negroes!!! Couldn't see past (the bag). Negotiation could have taken place, and you would have been in charge (black people), But y'all punk asses were too worried about losing a bag instead of standing up for your black asses, your family, and your pride and for all that black people stand for! That was one of your biggest mistakes ever. You might have a lot of money, and you might be millionaires, but you're still working for a white man who is a billionaire or trillionaire, and when he says shut up and dribble, or he says shut up and throw the pass, you do it. You're not independent, you're still working, and you're still enslaved, and that's the sad part. If your ignorant asses would have stood in solidarity and walked off the field, the basketball court, and the pitcher's mound, it could have been a whole new game with you (Black Folks in Charge).

The music industry is the same crap. How are non-black people in control of the hip-hop world? Can somebody explain that to me? But if that solidarity stand had taken place in the Sports Arena, then the blueprint would have been made. Then, people would know how to use the template and negotiate stuff. They just never got the memo, that **WE** are stronger in numbers and unity and solidarity than every other culture. The only time we're up in arms and come out in droves is to walk the streets in protest, then it dies down, and you go back to your daily bull shit. Guess what, take a STAND! Lose your (bag) for once, and we can renegotiate, we can hire black owners, we can buy our own team, we can do this, we can do that, but none of you ignorant asses couldn't figure that out. That's sad. I used to like Shaquille. I never liked Charles Barkley, but the more I listen to and see these black men on television bringing down other black men because they sold their souls getting paid by (the powers that be,) makes me nauseous. The buffoonery of it all. And again, all of the subliminal stuff that they do and put on

THE DREAM

television, and it goes right above our heads most of the time. It's sad. Think about it - they're starting to get the darkest of black men to become the spokesperson for something. And we don't even know we're being bamboozled. We're thinking we see a black man on television that we can relate to. We think we can identify with them or that we're getting more exposure. Or, in the political world, we see these dark guys like Tim Scott or Herschel Walker run for offices, and we're thinking, well, we're moving up, we're in the fight. It's all a hoax. It's all crap. Politics is an old white man's game, and it will never change. Unless the whole system is torn down and built back up again, it ain't changing. But, y'all can be hopeful and vote Democrat if you want to "Keep hope alive." I guess that's your slogan, right?

I was sixteen years old when I realized that old white America didn't give a shit about my black ass. I worked hard and accomplished everything I had and needed to do for me. I'm a black man first, and all the other labels that people tend to give me, it is what it is. But name me one black law that has been passed in the last five years for BLACK PEOPLE? Because I can't think of any. I know an Asian law has passed. Five Asians got beat up, and all of a sudden, there's Anti-Asian law for that. We black folks have been getting beat up and shot

THE DREAM

in the back, all kinds of craziness, and no anti-black law has been passed. We watched George Floyd get killed on TV, and billions of people saw that. Has that law been passed? I know a gay law has been passed. But old-ass Joe Biden is y'all's buddy. Every person, every culture that's non-black that comes into the United States has surpassed us tenfold. Stop me when I'm lying. We're always on the bottom of the totem pole because when you stand for nothing, you fall for anything. Tis is our motto! Throw us a crumb, and we's soo Happy Master! Ugh. The ironic part is every time they (the powers that be) try to do something to destroy us, the black population, with the drugs, the diseases, whatever they make up and put out there... evil has no boundaries, and it always flows over to their own just like AIDS. They were acting like that was a gay thing and a black thing. But then, when it started affecting the upper echelon, the elite, the Hollywood types, then they wanted to make a big deal like they gave a shit. Crack cocaine was inundated throughout the United States and placed in all the projects and hoods. Mostly black and brown areas, but guess what? All the suburban middle-class and upper-class whites were going into the hood to get the crack cocaine, and then it spread like wildfire. It's really funny, but a lot of times, the upper-class snobs always think that they have blind borders or barriers or something and they're untouchable, but when it comes to a disease, a drug, or anything that they (the government) (the powers that be) make up in a lab, they put in black neighborhoods to get rid of us. It always seeps out because hatred, disease, drugs, guns, racism, and all those things see no color. So, eventually, it will circle back around and get the exact people who put it out there. So now it's in your neighborhoods as well, karma's a bitch!!

JOEY

I'm going to a buddy of mine's 75th birthday party this afternoon. We've been friends for over 30 something years. We had lost touch for quite a few years because he was dealing with depression, and I kept reaching out. I didn't get a response, so I stopped calling, but I always kept tabs on him. Through a close girlfriend of his, I asked about him constantly and told her to give him my love and that I was praying for him. Mental health is real, and we need to adhere to it and handle it.

Well, he came to my first book signing, and I was very ecstatic, so we reconnected. Joey and I met, like I said, over 30 years ago at Charlie's West in the late '80s. If you remember, I mentioned that there was another club adjacent to the parking lot of Charlie's West called Boggie's. A fun straight club. So Joey was with his friend Karin at that club, and I guess he decided to come to Charlie's for a drink. We were all from St Clair Township, so I knew Karin. She introduced me to Joey and asked if I wouldn't mind dropping him off at home, and that's how we became fast friends. "So, Joey. What do you do in St. Clair?" I asked. "I own a hair salon," he replied. I was trying to make small talk and get to know him, but the music was really loud. He was feeling pretty good, and it was hard to talk, so I asked him if he wanted to dance. He agreed, and boy, did we dance. That's one thing we had in common: we love to dance.

Joey was a great dancer. He was a very good-looking man with jet-black hair and piercing blue eyes. Very jazzy dresser, and he favored Richard Gere, actually, the actor. Well, we closed the bar, and we were headed back to

St Clair. Well, by now, you know me. I was in my twenties. He was good-looking, he could dance, and I was attracted to him. I'm not sure if he invited me to stay over or if I suggested it. I think I probably suggested it because I was driving Papa's car, and I didn't want to walk home because I lived about 15 to 20 minutes away, and he was right up the street. So, it made more sense for me to stay there. And, like I said, he was attractive, and I was horny. We were both drunk, so we ended up fooling around just once. We became really dear friends and were simply not sexually compatible. We wanted the same thing. We were two alcoholics, having fun and living our best lives, and of course, we didn't know it at the time; at least I didn't. But we were going out five to seven days a week and slowly killing ourselves. In hindsight, he passed out, and I would drive home from the club, so it was a problem. But we had great times. We lived and learned. We are both clean and sober now, so that's a good thing!!! But man, we used to party our asses off. Joey was an entrepreneur. He had a very art deco salon in St Clair Township on South Park. He had a shop there for over 25 or 30 years, so he was very successful. He was also an antique guy. I think he still does that very part-time. I'm just very grateful that we reconnected.

FULL CIRCLE

Let me just tell you how God works: I was blessed to have my 62nd birthday party and take a cruise with an old buddy of mine, Joey. We reconnected after 15 years of not seeing each other. He had never been on a cruise before, and cruises are my favorite vacation, so we decided to go. We had the best time, and we plan to go on one this year. But the goodness of God and how he works is I'm in DC with a client of mine, and we're talking and telling each other about different vacations and how we love cruises and blah blah blah. Then, he mentioned this 12-day adventure Cruise in Africa that he's going on in a couple of weeks. "I want to go," was all I could say. Now, mind you, I just came back from a cruise at the end of November. I had a birthday party. My credit card was at the limit, but this was a vacation and a dream come true. A 12-day cruise from Mauritius to Cape Town, South Africa, With five ports of call in between. Listen, people: you just don't understand how crazy and magical life could be. Just look at the front cover of the book you're reading, and that will show you that dreams do come true. I thought of this cover and the map of Africa on August 23rd, 2023, and I sent it to the editor. Now, I'm headed on a cruise to the motherland!!! You just have to believe. I am back, and I had a wonderful time. Thanks, Eli, you're the man. Unfortunately, the pictures are not going to make the book because I have a deadline, and I'm hoping and praying that everything is completed in a few weeks because I'm having a book signing for the final book of the trilogy "THE DREAM" on May 4th, 2024.

THE DREAM

Yes, live the American dream if you think racism doesn't exist and Black lives don't matter...

Yes, live the American dream if you think the political structure gives a shit about poor people.

Yes, Live the American dream if you think this wasn't a systemic and systematic Ploy from the beginning...

Well, I've been living this so-called American Dream, and it's a fucking **Nightmare**!! But now, I'm woke. So I'm living my dream. Not what the powers that be Dictate. I'm taking my life into my own hands and living how I see fit with my rules. My Determination, My Destination, My Peace of Mind until the end of time!!! Because (YOUR DREAMS) can come TRUE…

Made in the USA
Monee, IL
22 April 2024